Vedika Kanchan

THE NEW

F

WORD

~ Essays on ~
Feminism and Women's Rights

EBD

EMBASSY BOOKS
www.embassybooks.in

This edition first published in 2018

Published in India by:
Embassy Book Distributors
120, Great Western Building,
Maharashtra Chamber of Commerce Lane,
Fort, Mumbai - 400 023.
Tel : (91-22) 22819546 / 22818567.
Email : info@embassybooks.in
Website : www.embassybooks.in

Distribution Centres:
Mumbai, Bangalore, Kolkata, Chennai,
Hyderabad, New Delhi, Pune

ISBN: 978-93-88247-00-9

Page Design and Layout by PSV Kumarasamy

Printed and Bound in India by Repro India Ltd., India

To all women who have felt less than -
Your voice matters.

Foreword

I grew up in Mumbai, with parents who always made it clear to me, in letter, spirit and action, that women and men are equal. Whether it is in cognitive intelligence, emotion, ambition, character or the ability to parachute off a cliff, the only differences between men and women are physical. Gender, according to them, cannot be a point of comparison. Men and women cannot be viewed in terms of superiority just because that is a perspective normalized by society. In my world, gender is not a weakness.

While they shaped my understanding of gender equality and feminism, my experiences illustrated a very different point of view, directing me to the dated attitudes that go unchallenged. Teachers that won't let boys cry on the pretext of masculinity, aunts with subtle suggestions to behave more lady-like, strangers that insist we "tone down" the feminist rhetoric are all among the thousand reasons to question the foundation that our world rests on.

About the time I was in the eighth grade, I started reading Virginia Woolf, and became incredibly intrigued by feminism and why women's rights are denied. I recall being transported to each wave, as the stories of feminists unfolded. Unfortunately, not many shared this interest. The cries of patriarchy silenced the voices that fought for women.

What started as a protest by Roman women against the resistance of consul Marcus Porcius Cato protesting laws that limited a women's right to use expensive goods, in 3rd century BCE, is now a global movement, demanding the equality of the sexes, known as Feminism.

In waves, it has been reduced to just being about women's rights.

Feminism, however, is about equality for both men and women. The dictionary defines it as:

noun

The advocacy of women's rights on the ground of the equality of the sexes.

Britannica takes it a step further with:

Feminism, *the belief in the social, economic, and political equality of the sexes. Although largely originating in the West, feminism is manifested worldwide and is represented by various institutions committed to activity on behalf of women's rights and interests.*

There may be many people pursuing their personal agendas, masquerading themselves as feminists. Misunderstood, misconstrued, mocked and reviled, Feminism continues to face barriers at all ends. In a largely embattled world, that also stands polarized on a variety of issues of grave concern, we need to have one less theatre of war.

In this set of essays, I attempt to illustrate my perspective towards Feminism, how it impacts lives and the misconceptions that surround a pivotal world movement. The chapters ahead synthesize perspective and ideas surrounding women rights.

Stay with me here!

*"For most of history,
anonymous was a woman"*
– Virginia Woolf

A Little Bit of History

While this hasn't been officially recorded or accepted, many believe that the history of feminism emanated from Cleopatra's bold succession and rule in ancient Egypt. At the same time, historians, world wide, mark the first feminist dissent at the entrance of the Forum at Capitoline Hill, with women protesting Marcus Cato's decision in 3rd century BCE.

Feminism and the feminist movement (as we, perhaps, know it) is rooted in 14th- and early 15th-century France when Christine de Pisan insisted that a woman is worth more than her beauty. She championed the importance of education for women and insisted that the world change the way it perceived gender. Her goal was to reverse misogynistic mindsets; she wanted to make it such that women were seen as more than vessels of reproduction or slaves to their men. A woman was more than a wife. This call for action drove into the end of the 16th century with women like Laura Cereta, Moderata Fonte, Mary Astell, Heinrich Cornelius Agrippa, Modesta di Pozzo di Forzi,

Marie Le Jars de Gournay, Anne Bradstreet, Francois Poullain de la Barre and many others who voiced their protesting opinion against the mistreatment of women, forced marriages for the sake of family status, and the belief that women were not worthy of education and, specifically lower class women must be separated from their aristocrat counterparts.

Of course, this wasn't taken too well. Women were cast as superficial, trivial, objects, and a multitude of undesirable characteristics. On the other hand, emerging feminists, at the time, produced laundry lists of women with courage and accomplishment. They proclaimed that women would be intellectual equals of men if they were given equal access to education and as democratization took hold, the right to vote, the right to work, and the right to be treated as human.

Since then, there have been what are known as the three "waves" of feminism. The first wave in the nineteenth and early twentieth centuries focused heavily on a woman's right to vote. The second wave beginning in the 1960s focused on women's liberation and their legal and social rights for women. The third wave aimed to pick on what were considered failures of second-wave feminism and began in the 1990s.

Let's start from the beginning.

The First Wave of Feminism

During the Renaissance period, women were perceived as silly, frivolous, irrational creatures, born subordinate to men. French philosopher Jean-Jacques Rousseau portrayed women as inferior in his works. In fact, when French revolutionaries published the *Declaration of the Rights of Man and of the Citizen*, a document arguing for fair treatment and equality, they disregarded the legal status of women. Though hypocritical, the double standards were not surprising. However, this directed a volley of writing towards the idea that women were equal to men, as worthy as men and as rational as men. In response to the French revolutionaries, Olympe de Gouges published the *Declaration of the Rights of Woman and of the [Female] Citizen* which sharply called out French society for its unfair treatment of women and forced change. Accordingly, in *A Vindication of the Rights of Women*, Mary Wollstonecraft's challenged the notion that women existed for the sole purpose of pleasing a man. She asked for equal opportunities towards women and men in education, work, and politics. She argued for women to be treated as equals of men, with the same capabilities and rights. In that vein, Wollstonecraft once wrote, "if women are silly, it is only because society trains them to be irrelevant." She criticized the idea that women were weak and went ahead to say that women tend to "cultivate" weaknesses to appear pleasing to men.

The Age of Enlightenment, beset by revolutions across Europe, presented the world with developments in the arts, philosophy and politics. While this popularized the socialization of abolitionism, it influenced the feminist movement differently. For the first time, feminist activists across North America and Europe exchanged ideas, demanded that their voices be heard and protested for freedom, rights and equality.

The first Women's Rights Convention was held in 1848. Elizabeth Cady Stanton, one of the five women who initiated this, used the *Declaration of Independence* as the foundation for the *Declaration of Sentiments*. *The Declaration of Sentiments* guided the Seneca Falls Convention where she drafted eleven resolutions, including one that gave women the right to vote, a radical notion at the time. However, even when women achieved platforms and created, for themselves, opportunities where their voices were heard, they were stalled by men who remained unconvinced. Nevertheless, all eleven resolutions were passed. In particular, the biggest win for Stanton, and women around the world was an approval "for the overthrowing of the monopoly of the pulpit, and for securing equal participation of women and men various trades, professions and commerce."

The Suffrage Movement saw many women rise for a woman's right to vote in national and local elections – the cause of equality. While advocates of the suffrage movement saw the right to vote as the stamp of equality and freedom, radical feminists like Emma Goldman challenged the power of the ballot as the foundation for equality. She emphatically professed that women would gain their freedom "by refusing the right to anyone over her body...by refusing to be a servant to God, the state, society, the husband, the family, etc., by making her life simpler but deeper and richer." In her work, *Women and Economics,* Charlotte Perkins Gilman ardently pushed for women to be liberated from the "domestic mythology" of home. They argued that a woman was not tied to her family and that they were forced to depend on men even when they truly wanted to be independent and free.

All this emphasis on education and political rights, however, was the prerogative of women of the upper classes and the elite. Ordinary women, especially single, non-white ones, with not as many means, were not adequately, if at all, represented. Bearing this mind, a voice that channeled such injustices and spoke for underrepresented women was Sojourner Truth, a former slave. She was a symbol of the chasm between the ordinary and the privileged. She famously questioned those before the Women's Rights Convention in Akron, Ohio, "That man over there says that women need to be helped into carriages, and lifted over ditches, and to have the best place everywhere. Nobody ever helps me into carriages, or over mud-puddles, or gives me any best place! And ain't I a woman?"

However, the Civil War in America and repression in Europe placed the focus on women's rights on the backburner. The efforts, and voices, became feeble. These were re-ignited in 1903 when British Suffragist Emmeline Pankhurst broke free of the current manner of lobbying and took the movement to a more violent form with a series of bombings and boycotting. This led to a nation-wide movement and the British Parliament was compelled to extend voting rights to women householders, householders' wives, and female university graduates over the age of 30 in 1918. Alice Paul, influenced by this, followed the tactics in the United States and organized mass demonstrations, confrontations with the police, very public acts of civil disobedience, *en masse*, and took her argument and journal-led movement into the face of public violence. In 1920, their efforts were rewarded, and they emerged triumphant with the passing of the 19th Amendment to the American Constitution.

Once women gained the right to vote, the feminist movement lost momentum. It became weak in face of uncertainty. This time, there was no one common agenda to "fight" for. The movement itself splintered into many groups, none of which stood up for the rights that extend beyond suffrage, both in Europe and in the United States. Groups like the Women's Joint Congressional Committee who lobbied to bring in legislation to promote education, maternal and infant health care; the Women's Trade Union League that worked towards protective labor legislation for women; the League of Women Voters that organized voter registration and education worked around their chosen areas of focus. None of these, however, was strongly "feminist" in nature.

As a result, the post-suffrage world, saw a vacuum emerge in the feminist movement. Alicia Paul, leading the National Woman's Party, at this time chose to focus on bringing in an Equal Rights Amendment (ERA) to ensure women were not discriminated against and were treated equally by law. This did not go down too well with many groups as they were not exactly looking for absolute equality. A lot of them were looking at straight benefits to, and protective legislation like mandating eight hours only shifts for women. Paul, however, pointed out the myopic view this brought in: she highlighted that if that legislation went through, it would force employers to hire fewer women as they would prove to be expensive resources. Across the sea, Aletta Jacobs from the Netherlands and Beatrice Webb of England raised their voices in demand for equality and opposed protective legislation for women just as vociferously as Paul.

Advocates of the pro-protective legislation, however, opposed this strongly, raising questions on the very nature, essence and goal of feminism. They voiced their fears around equality at the cost of a protection, a support structure that was vital for so many.

Interestingly, across both the United States and Europe, many believed that women had achieved liberation because they were allowed to vote in the same manner that men were.

Before this could be debated and disproved,

the world suffered tragedies of immense measure, first by the Great Depression and then by World War II. As unfortunate as these circumstances were, World War II opened up work opportunities for women as men were conscripted into the army, many never to return. From working in a variety of factories to playing professional sports, women were presented with the opportunities that they didn't even dream of before.

All of this, of course, changed when the war ended, and men returned back home. The general mood became one of domestication. More men and women wanted to be married at a relatively young age. Domesticity seemed to be the new culture. Women's employment numbers were lower in 1960 than they were in 1930.

Of course, this idealism did not last long.

The Second Wave of Feminism

Extensive debates and discourse around the nature and principles of gender, equality, discrimination and justice, protests against the Vietnam War, discussions about the role of a family characterized the next wave of feminism. It made its presence felt around the same time as The Civil Rights Movement.

The President's Commission on the Status of

Women led by Eleanor Roosevelt reported the benefits of nuclear families as well as highlighted employment discrimination, unequal pay, legal inequality, and meagre support services for working women throughout the country. The report recommended correcting these through legislative guarantees of equal pay for equal work, equal job opportunities, and expanded child-care services. This ushered in the Equal Pay Act of 1963 that offered the first guarantee. The Civil Rights Act of 1964 was amended to bar employers from discriminating on the basis of sex.

However, women were continually denied free access to contraception, job openings were still segregated by gender and rape and domestic violence continued, unreported.

At that accord, the splintering of feminism continued.

National Organization for Women (NOW) focused on legal equity. Smaller groups raised their voices for a multitude of reasons – from demanding the inclusion of female authors in university curriculum to demanding establishment of rape crises centers to advocating the right to not be referred to by their marital status to repealing protective laws.

Women now achieved positions that had been unavailable to them for decades including posts as pilots, soldiers, bus drivers, bankers, soldiers, professional sports players and everything a 14th century woman couldn't begin to imagine. Children's books were re-written, as were college curricula. Women's studies departments were created in universities and colleges worth their salt.

On the downside, too many activists were doing too many things and debating too many ideologies. An inclusive, all-encompassing feminist ideology was sorely missing. The questions were easy to ask. It was the answers that led to deep divides to the extent of not even having one common definition of feminism, or liberation, or equality that all could agree on. Many competing tracts of feminism emerged.

There were "Anarcho-feminists," who went the Emma Goldman path and said that women could not be liberated without questioning the function, nature and essence of institutions such as the family, private property, and state power. There were Individualist feminists, who raised the call for minimal government intervention to solve women's problems. "Amazon feminists" advocated liberation through physical strength. Separatist feminists raised the flag for liberation through separation from men for some period.

However, all of these continued to merge and disrupt, sometimes to the point of bringing other women down.

From these, three major streams of thought surfaced.

Liberal, or mainstream, feminism focused its energy on concrete change at an institutional and governmental level. It aimed to ensure equal access for women to positions previously considered the domain of men. This stream strove for evident measures as equal number of women and men in positions of power, or an equal amount of money spent on male and female student-athletes, along with ensuring the present-day form of protective legislation such as special workplace benefits for maternal leave. As a whole, it is a forward moving outlook on women's rights.

In sharp contrast, radical feminism wanted to reshape the inherent and rampant patriarchal society that guided institutions. They argued that unless society redesigned itself in a revolutionary manner, the close stitches of the subservient role that women played in society would never be removed from the social fabric. Their beliefs and actions were geared towards reducing traditional power relationships to a more equal footing. At the same time, they sought to develop inclusive, hierarchy-free approaches to politics and organization.

Cultural or "difference" feminism, the last of the three streams, advocated celebrating the qualities of women that differentiated them from men, such as their greater concern for affective relationships and their focus on nurturing others. This arm of feminism negated the attempts to make women more like men. And, in this process, they offered a critique of attempts to storm traditionally male spheres.

Another issue besetting even the second wave of feminism was the exclusion of non-white women – whether or not educated. The ambivalence created towards their "middle class, white problems," in the minds of women from other races, classes and stations stalled the possible strengthening of the second wave of feminism.

While the campaign against employment and wage discrimination helped reduce some of this tension across the class divide, feminism for African American women continued to go through its own tumult. Women in racial minorities were caught between the crosshairs of having to get their privileged counterparts to think about racial issues and men to think about gender issues.

Prominent names like Michele Wallace, Mary Ann Weathers, Alice Walker, and Bettina Aptheker raised these issues in their own ways. Toni Cade Bambara questioned in *The Black Woman: An Anthology*, "How relevant are the truths, the experiences, the findings of White women to Black women? I don't know that our priorities are the same, that our concerns and methods are the same." She, and others, echoed whispers and shouts from as far back as Sojourner Truth, that feminists with different backgrounds were incapable of understanding their challenges.

The commonalities to battle out, of course, remained daycare, abortion, maternity leave, violence. On these common and specific issues, African American feminists and Caucasian feminists built tentative, yet, effective working relationships.

As they neared the end of the 20th century, fledgling feminist movements of Asia, Africa, and Latin America started interacting with European and American feminists. A whole new world opened up as feminists from developed countries began to realize the realities faced by women in other parts of the world. While some fancied themselves the liberators of "Third World" women, their understanding of the fabric of these lives was so little that more often than not the solutions they "provided" were at loggerheads with the realities of women in these regions. This was so much so, that many international conferences saw women from Third World countries actively dissenting the hijacking of these agendas by American and European activists to further their own. Azizah al-Hibri, a law professor and scholar of Muslim women's rights chastised them during the 1994 International Conference on Population and Development, in Cairo, saying "[Third World women] noted that they could not very well worry about other matters when their children were dying from thirst, hunger or war. The conference instead centered around reducing the number of Third World babies in order to preserve the earth's resources, despite (or is it 'because of') the fact that the First World consumes much of these resources."

Towards the end of the 20th century, feminism was going through whirlpools.

The eradication of female directed violence in certain parts of Africa and the ban on child marriage and widow burning in India in the 20th century saw the start of many women's rights wins. However, at the same time, it also saw horrifyingly backwards gender norms that forced women to forgo their education, in favor of serving their men.

From increasing dissonance over the use of sexist language, women in sports, divorce laws that were fair to women, entry of women into organized religion, to ecofeminism (a philosophical and political theory and movement which combines ecological concerns with feminist ones, regarding both as resulting from male domination of society), the Western World continued to see the influence of feminism advance by many degrees.

However, part of the reality is that feminism, at a global level, was far from uniform. The way that cultural feminists pursued feminism was very different from those who idolize mainstream feminists. Women in different parts of India were treated differently from women in various parts of Europe. African American women on the east coast faced barriers that were poles apart from those faced by women in Nairobi or Buenos Aires.

Economic, political and cultural differences across the globe accentuated these differences and, as a result, made one international forum and one solution to fit all impossible.

The Third Wave of Feminism

All of this global tumult and uncertainty led to the flow of the third wave of feminism in the mid-1990s. Born in the age of media saturation, cultural and economic diversity, on the bedrock of the economic, professional and political power achieved by women in the second wave, and where women now have significant legal rights and protections, Generation X (as they are popularly called) critiqued the loose ends of their predecessors' work. The information revolution allowed for a massive change in communication and, thus, wider and greater dissemination and exchange of ideas in the late 20th century.

The postmodernist movement influenced feminist in the third wave to demand change even in the definitions of the ideas, words, and portrayal of what it meant to be a woman, of gender, beauty, masculinity, femininity and sexuality. The understanding of gender itself went through a mutli-level scanner. Were there strict lines of demarcation between gender? How about considering that in every individual there are some characteristics that are strictly male and others that are strictly female? This paved the path to the concept of a gender continuum. Now, each human being could be seen as having, expressing, displaying and even suppressing the entire range of traits that had previously been considered strictly the ownership of one gender or the other.

Third-wave feminists, therefore, took "sexual liberation," a critical focus area of the second-wave to a new process of owning their gender identity – one needed to first be aware of what shaped their gender identity and sexual orientation and then taking the ownership to freely express ones "authentic gender identity."

While the first wave of feminism was very focused on Suffrage and the second wave worked on a variety of (non-aligned) areas, the Third Wave, of which the Third Wave Foundation, founded by Rebecca Walker (the daughter of second-wave activist Alice Walker) with others was a prominent group, channeled their energies to supporting "groups and individuals working towards gender, racial, economic, and social justice".

Leading feminists in the third wave, daughters of the second wave feminists, had been fed a healthy diet of examples of female success, high expectations of success and achievement, heightened awareness of the obstacles of gender, race and class. Their battle cry, thus, became one of sabotaging the existing system (of sexist, classist, racist symbols, patriarchy, violence, and continued exclusion in many areas) and building a new one.

Women now started turning the tables on the

status quo. What was considered derogatory and demeaning slang became labels proudly worn. Conversations previously held behind closed doors in hushed tones now spilled out into the social fabric. Eve Ensler's play *The Vagina Monologues* boldly explored women's feelings and takes on sexuality that included sexuality-centred topics as diverse as orgasms, birth, and rape. The Riot Grrls movement protested against male dominance in the music scene and encouraged women to create their own music rather than following and imitating what existed. They used music to express their feminist views. The Guerrilla Girls, feminists who wore gorilla masks in public kept the focus on issues of gender and ethnic bias as well as corruption in politics, art, film, and pop culture. Believers of intersectional feminism that fought discrimination on the basis of caste, gender, ethnicity, the Guerrilla Girls canvassed for human rights for all people and genders.

The third wave, inclusive of women and girls of colour, worked to paint an assertive, powerful and in-control picture of women and girls. No longer were women to be subject to stereotypes of meek and submissive. Icons as famous as Madonna, Queen Latifah and Oprah Winfrey dominated the music and media scene. Women depicted in media – TV and movies as well as children's programmes – were independent, smart and powerful.

The internet – and ease of exchanging information, thoughts and ideas through blogs – brought forth third-wave feminist points of view to a larger audience. It can easily be said that the internet served to democratize the focus of the feminist movement. It allowed for a global outreach, increased and enlarged participation, highlighted issues spoken about as well as ideated for solutions based on the reality of where the audience was from.

Of course, like any other era and wave, the third wave too had its critics. Even before it had fully found its feet, some critics were arguing that the movement had lived its usefulness and could now be rested. Feminists from the second wave debated that the issues remained the same, not much had changed and all that the next generation had done was nothing. They, along with critics of the third wave, demanded to know whether debating provocative clothing, transforming pole dancing into a form of exercise, choosing to stay single and initiating divorce proceedings truly represented sexual liberation.

In what seems to be the onset of the next wave of feminism, a whole new set of rules and credos seem to be emerging. It will be interesting to see what this new wave of feminism will look like.

Table of Contents

"You may shoot me with your words,
You may cut me with your eyes,
You may kill me with your hatefulness,
But still, like air, I'll rise."

– Maya Angelou

1

The New F Word

The Controversy behind "Feminism" and the Barriers to Women's Rights

"Feminism" elicits images as far back as the bra-burning 60s and as recent as "#ShePersisted. However, even in the wake of this cultural metamorphosis, misinterpretation orchestrates a blistered stereotype. Instead of equality, "feminism" is perceived as a representation of man-haters and spite, so much so that women around the world reject the movement entirely. In this parade of conflicting interpretations, "feminism" is charged with unrelenting stigma. Though the idea of women's rights is matched with programs and actions that contribute to a more equal world, women's rights continue to remain challenged to those that rise for it.

Whether it is sexist school dress codes, catcalling at construction sites – or even outside of construction sites, thinly veiled 'suggestions' about how to behave in a more "lady-like" manner, or segregated PE lessons, our actions today are products of a world that believes men are more deserving than women. However, a sexist attitude is also a grave injustice to boys. We teach boys to strangle their compassion to preserve masculinity. We ask them to fear vulnerability and lionize superficial strength, misidentifying their emotions as a weakness. We then deal a worse hand to girls because we teach them to humor this hyper-masculinity.

This reality is not limited to our personal lives. The feminist perspective is also essential in international relations. More specifically, in terms of policy making and peace initiatives, the plight of women's rights is heavily ignored.

The development of laws after violent conflicts in multiple contexts around the world treats women's rights struggles as second to military achievement. There remains, therefore, a polarized focus on protecting women in the context of their relationship with others rather than as individuals. By discounting these underlying conflicts, post-conflict laws have been unable to tackle the issue of gender inequality at a more permanent level, rendering them inapplicable in a modern scenario. This does not merely emulate gross neglect of human rights but also the systematic objectification of women into *'conquerable'* property – a bitter truth that continues to plague our society with rape and other atrocities in the present. It is this atmosphere and this historical context that perpetuates ingrained biases of women as inferior and allows for physical, emotional and sexual assault in the world today.

This is especially true considering how far consent is misinterpreted. Women, around the world, are perceived as gears of reproduction, removed from the rights they are promised on the basis of being human. As these attitudes become normalized, they blur the lines that define consent. At that accord, the stigmas attached to sex, make it even more difficult for these lines to be clarified. As a result, we breed a population of men that are ignorant towards the importance of consent, making women convenient scapegoats for repressed frustrations.

Bearing this in mind, it is frightening that our society perceives women only in the context of their relationship with men. When a woman is assaulted, we argue that she was wronged and must receive justice because she is "someone's sister, wife or daughter." She was wronged and must receive justice because she is human. It is dangerous to argue that a woman is only worth respect when it damages her family's integrity. It is even more dangerous that women who have been assaulted are pounded with a laundry list of questions, suggesting that their words, actions or clothes were provocative.

Today, more than ever, in a world as interconnected, inter-woven and embattled as ours, we need to start paying more attention to the importance of equality between men and women.

Being treated as an equal to a man should not make a woman lucky; it should make them human. The fundamental rights of women have morphed into rare advantages such that gender equality is now a privilege.

It is unsurprising that polarized battle hymns compress a movement this spectral under a blemished umbrella term. Feminism is loosely applied to a host of movements and ideas, almost disregarding the weight of gender equality. At that length, sexism, feminism, the battle for equality and breaking the glass ceiling are not the same. However, they are used with little concern of the implications that follow.

Is this war against cookie-cutter images viable? Even at the cost of the Feminist Mystique losing its household familiarity?

Why is feminism the new F word?

"We are struggling for a uniting word
but the good news is that
we have a uniting movement."

– Emma Watson

Fourth Wave?

Social Media and 21st century Feminism

Many of us draw our identities from feminist dimensions, while others shy away. Some may say that sexism doesn't exist, that 18th century constructs are obsolete. Is any society in this world ever truly obliterated of prejudice?

In Technopoly, a novel composed of discourse that defines technology, Neil Postman wrote, "A bargain is struck [when new technology is established] in which technology giveth and technology taketh away." If Postman is to be believed, then the value posed by social media is symmetrical only to its price.

21st century media has made it such that

anyone can rally their thoughts, unbridled, on a global scale. Unlike print, social media does not force political correctness nor does it pay lip service (or genuine consideration) to conflicting thoughts. In the age of information and technology, news is available at our fingertips and plays a huge role in molding public opinion. Anyone is free to voice their (often unfiltered) thoughts, write what they please and champion their opinions without the fear of being questioned into silence. This bravado, and if I may go out on a limb here to say so, arrogance, is also rooted in the anonymity that social media affords us. As users hide under the guise of a username, they become less likely to reel in their views. By doing so, they are free to convey their ideas because the consequences bear no marks.

In the wake of this dynamic, women and men find themselves capable of conveying 'man-hating' or 'women exalting' ideas, masked as "feminism." Without having to account for their words, without having to justify their claims with hard data and evidence, and without any course correction seeped in facts and empathy, their ideas are viewed as the truth.

Not only has this given activism a boost, but it also has made it possible for popular opinion to start influencing governance and policy, giving the average citizen a voice in pressing social matters. Whether this is slander, misogynistic rants infesting the world with prejudice or radicalized agendas masquerading as faith, the ability to spread unsubstantiated claims misuses social media's expressive value. Today, parading ideas at a global level comes at no cost. So, when extremist views do come into play, it is not difficult for them to be broadcasted on a colossal scale. This stands particularly true for the feminist movement. It is not surprising that social media has played a role in stigmatizing feminism.

Not only has it been easy to express conflicting interpretations of feminism, but it has also been easy to spread these views. Misinterpretations of feminism are not expressed in isolation. Rather, these ideas have gathered support and a following, not only in men but also in women. These factors have combined to normalize opinions against feminism and make it seem as if feminists hate men. In turn, feminist views have developed a reputation for being highly disputed and, often, extremist.

This dynamic is especially true given the growth of democratic values. As the world moves closer towards these values, freedom of speech and freedom of the press have become paramount. The importance of freedom, in both respects, has further armed men and women (as it should) to convey their thoughts freely. The flip side of this coin is that in doing so, these ideas have also highlighted opinions that rest at the other end of the spectrum. Regrettably, it is the negative interpretation of feminism that has gained particular attention. As these ideas spread, "feminism" reaches the height of the controversy. Women and men have now become hesitant to adopt the "feminist" label, even in light of its considerable drive for equality. The implications of this seep into society in the most inconspicuous form.

By swarming fact with propagandist fiction, social media's expanse of communication maneuvers public sentiments – granting offenders the power to influence the easily swayed, inadvertently or otherwise. One has to, therefore, wonder if this freedom of expression can be too "free" – if a platform championed for its autonomy and uncensored liberty actually creates more misinformation and misunderstanding. Such platforms have the ability to not only transform mass communication, but eclipse conventional media outlets. It is at this point that the degree of misinformation becomes truly perilous.

As beaten of a cliché as it is, there is truth to the idea of "history repeating itself." Actions molding the shape of global relations are reactions perpetuating cycles of upheaval and battle. Our society continues to seek a glimpse into the future, peering down the peephole to ascertain what happens next. We flounder for an understanding of what the world will be. It is, therefore, through learning from the peaks and pits of our past that we can glimpse the state of our future. Ideally, a study of history allows us to alter our world – especially if we don't see light shining at the end of our tunnel. This is necessary when we look at the feminist movement.

 The word feminism is not exclusive to women. Some of the most impactful feminists I've known have been men – my father, my teachers, and even my 17-year-old male friends. It is vital to understand feminism for what it is: an intersection of justice to both men and women.

As we combat gender stereotypes, we not only hope for women to be CEOs or wear a tuxedo to prom, but also for a man to raise children without being perceived as inferior; or for a boy to carry a Hello Kitty backpack without being called a girl.

The stigma associated with feminism is not new. Through the years the challenges have changed, but the stereotypes have remained the same. The very reason that feminism exists is that there is something wrong with the status quo, with the balance that our world needs. However, we have fallen into a pattern of stoicism where these injustices are let go.

This automatically places feminists in a position of conflict, regardless of where they are or what they experience. Feminists advocate for change in the present condition. Even though this change is positive, it is nonetheless, an approach which asks the world to deviate from reality as they know to be true. Through the course of history, this has made feminism questionable or misunderstood.

It is only recently that the stigmas have reversed: voices against women's rights are now marked with the same stigma that once approached their opponents. Rather than the concept of women's rights, it is the title of a feminist that creates problems. Voices against feminism still carry a following large enough to brand the movement as negative, something that has only escalated with 21st century media.

Nevertheless, many argue that feminism is not necessarily a proponent of equality. This is not to say that feminists do not strive for gender equality. However, there is a considerable difference between gender equality and feminism. While feminism advocates for women's rights, gender equality advocates for men and women to have access to rights, regardless of gender. Proponents of this theory argue that this makes feminism appear as if it is challenging men when in reality it is merely challenging the attitude that men are superior. With this female-centrism, it becomes easy for men and women to buy into the view that feminists hate men.

Another idea that holds equal weight is the belief that women are not disadvantaged, that men and women are on equal footing. Legally, there has been progress regarding women's rights; we underestimate the struggles in implementing them practically. It is true that the world has, admirably, fought to secure women's rights in politics, business and even at homes. However, it is in ordinary circumstances that women continue to be treated as second to men. In many parts of the world, the legal progress is outright reversed.

These problems are easy to ignore because they may seem trivial in light of the past. Many even believe that the women's rights struggle is imagined. To them, this makes feminism redundant. The danger of that, coupled with human behavior, makes us less likely to support a cause if we see it as unnecessary and, in turn, begin to question and challenge its proponents.

It is easy to detach ourselves from 'distant' issues when their significance in our world is misunderstood.

Despite the strong rhetoric of conflict resolution, there is an underlying reality we are continually shielded from. Some may even be hesitant to accept this because it asks them to confront the most unappealing aspects of society. By shielding ourselves from taboo topics, leaving things unsaid or merely choosing words with hard-hitting connotations, we change the way knowledge is perceived and shared.

However, educating ourselves about society requires us to confront its grotesque ideas. It implores us to recognize the truths and realities that make us uncomfortable, which would otherwise be easier to ignore.

Even when the relevance of feminism is clear, men may be unwilling to adopt the title. This may not be pure bigotry. Some would argue that it is the misunderstanding of machoism or masculinity that edges men away from feminism. The 'model' image of a man is often attached to the image of hyper-masculinity. Since feminism is assumed to be women-centric, the pressure of masculinity makes men hesitate to 'risk' their machoism for the sake of women's rights. It is this tough balancing act that gives rise to anti-feminist voices.

The idea of feminism is often approached with caution. Since its meaning is battered with misinterpretation, we find ourselves uneasy when asked if we adopt the values of feminism. These splintered approaches ultimately contribute to the stigma that is associated with feminism, marking it as the new F word.

*"Culture does not make people.
People make culture.
If it is true that the full humanity of
women is not our culture, then we
can and must make it our culture."*

– Chimamanda Ngozi Adichie

3

Women are from the West and Men are from Mars

Identity Politics and the Perception of Women's rights as Western rights

Though women's rights have developed across the world, certain groups of women and men are still unwilling to back the movement, choosing instead to keep to gender norms. While this may seem surprising, it reflects the choice to preserve group-identity and culture over genre equality. Many perceive women's rights as attached to the West. Due to this perception, they see supporting these rights as integrating with the Western culture and undermining their own.

That women's rights are primarily associated
with the West, is a perception arising due to
a lack of understanding between norms and
culture. Norms are defined, accepted, adhered
to and set social behavior that is standard.
Culture, on the other hand, is a smorgasbord
that comprises beliefs, values, customs *and*
norms that represent a society. It is true that
culture influences norms, but they are not the
same. This is the reason why we believe that
gender norms in certain parts of this world
are products of their culture. There is a divide
between women rights movements in the West
and the rest of the world: in many countries,
women and men are less sympathetic towards
women's rights if they believe that it *Westernizes*
them.

As the world becomes more globalized, ideas
and trends spread quickly across the globe,
including those from the Western world into
other parts of the world. Some cultures have,
thus, come to view the spread of these ideas
and trends as threats. While they do not *seek* to
undermine local culture and customs, Western
ideas are *seen to do* just that. This perspective
is rooted in the belief that culture is constant.
However, history has shown that cultures
around the world have changed and developed
in different ways. There is a sort of animosity

between the West and many different cultures. The hostility toward women's rights may well be a result of this perception.

As many countries rally for their own nationalist identity, parts of their society advocate for a rejection of Western culture as "morally loose." The inability to distinguish culture from rights results in a perception of losing self-identity or subverting national agendas. This serves as a barrier to any efforts by reinforcing gender roles and the image of the ideal woman as subservient.

The idea of women's rights struggles exists in a male-centered context. Even laws and literature describing rape place men at the center (and as a victim) of the conflict (by being portrayed as being wrongly targeted) rather than the female victims - thus, further robbing women of their voice.

This idea is reinforced when considered in light of identity and politics. It is undeniable that culture can be a part of identity, so much so that we tend to perceive any threat to our culture as a threat to the way we identify ourselves. Since gender norms are misconstrued to be part of culture, any deviations are seen as threats to identity. Identity politics makes this even more problematic. "Identity" has become formative to the political landscape to the extent that "national interests are rooted in identity and has emerged as an instrument of self-assertion. "Identity politics" is defined as the "tendency of people of the same interest to form broad political alliances." However, identity politics questions universal human rights: as cultural identities become more relevant to the political atmosphere, it becomes harder to adopt principles that are, falsely, associated with the West. Women are treated as cultural symbols rather than cultural actors, solely on behalf of false national identity. While human rights exist at a legal level, they are not implemented at an individual level.

Many argue that women's rights in the West are entirely different from women's rights in other parts of the world. While women's rights movements in the West lean towards shattering the glass ceiling, equal political representation, better divorce laws among other issues, women's rights movements in many parts of the rest of the world tend to focus on access to education or basic resources. It is argued that the problems women's rights movements in the West focus on, pale in comparison to those of the rest of the world. Since resources and education are seen as more urgent, they make it seem as if the self-professed 'Western' problems aren't truly problems at all. This further deepens the divide between both stands and makes women and men unwilling to adopt women's rights.

Though the imbalance makes it seem as if the West does not require women's rights movements as pertinently as the rest of the world, this is not exactly the case. For one, both domains are in different stages of the women's rights movement. Because the West has already achieved progress in terms of resources and education, it now has a chance to focus on different kinds of problems. This is given the regional and, largely, political stability that has allowed them to focus on these areas. Without having the threat of war or regional conflict, the West has been able to devote resources towards the cause of women's rights. Another explanation is that different parts of the world simply demand different concentrations. Given the varying racial, cultural and social dynamics, gender norms have developed in different ways, breeding their individual, unique set of problems. As such, a divide runs through the movement.

As far as the feminist movement goes, these divided ideas make it less urgent and important for governments to direct limited resources towards the issue. If the public itself is uncertain about the movement, governments have precious little motivating them to pursue these internal changes. Even if governments do support women's rights, without public acceptance of the movement, these will only exist at a theoretical level. It is challenging to translate women's rights from a theoretical to a practical level if the public is uncooperative.

Ultimately, this fosters an environment where women's rights are inexplicably tied to the West and, in that process, considered in light of the so-called danger it poses to culture, as opposed to the benefits it upholds for men and women. As these attitudes surface with greater ferocity than before, the rights we have already secured are also at threat.

Feminism, we must remember, anywhere in the world, is going to be necessary until we view women as humans, not daughters, sisters or wives, but people.

"I hate to hear you talk about all women as if they were fine ladies instead of rational creatures. None of us want to be in calm waters all our lives."

– Jane Austen, Persuasion

4

#Shero
#Girlboss
#Herstory

Gendered Language and
the Problem with Pronouns

Language has been heavily impacted by the
intricacies of sexism and gender equality.
Though this can be seen as a recent addition to
the network of interwoven gender dynamics,
it has also been a part of early women's rights
movements and dissent. Current avenues of
communication have made it such that language
has evolved to accommodate, and challenge, the
growing masses. Since we rely, so laboriously,

on quick and clear communication, we call for the progress in language, specifically the addition of words that welcome new ideas and phenomena. In terms of the women's rights movement, this has given rise to words like "girl boss," "mansplaining," and "Shero."

While this appears merely as a way to communicate, it has also reinforced gender distinctions. By branding specific genders with specific words, we bring light to the difference between both sexes. This propels the idea of women as separate – and unfortunately inferior - from men, rather than women and men united and equal.

In many ways, these words have emerged as a way for empowerment. By adding "girl" before "boss," women hope to "take back" words that are stereotypically associated with men. At the same time, they have also been used to fight back against everyday sexism. By configuring the term "mansplaining," women do not have to defend whether it exists. Since there is a name for circumstances where men explain women's issues to women in their own terms, there is little that people can say to deny that it exists. People find that by establishing a term for sexist behavior, they are also establishing that sexist behavior exists: it would not be necessary to contrive the word "mansplaining" if it was not common. The establishment of these words challenges existing gender roles and inspires changes in gender norms.

Changes in gender norms have driven changes in language. One such example is the use of pronouns such as 'they.'

Because "they" is used as a collective pronoun, using it in place of the singular "he" or "she" often translates to awkward grammatical structures. It is not easy for people to carry a word that they are uncomfortable using. While this makes many resistant to adopt "they," it also makes them unwelcoming to the changing gender norms "they" stands for.

The use of binary gender pronouns hosts similar problems. Due to the frequency with which they are used, binary pronouns become unintentional participants in the reinforcement of gender stereotypes. Whether it is in the fact that crime television shows refer to unknown criminals as a "he," a manager in the corporate world always referred to as a "he," or the assumption that a secretary is always a "she," binary gender pronouns allow for gender stereotypes to be made concrete.

Ironically, this is also true for the use of gender-neutral language in legal frameworks. Gender-neutral language is used with the intent of portraying equality. By using language which applies to both genders, it is implied that laws composed utilizing this language apply to both sexes as well. The idea that a law is universally applicable rests on the idea that all individuals carry universal conditions. In a world where women are often treated as second to men, this is not always the case. The weight of prejudice makes it difficult for theoretical equality to become real.

Sexism persists. Whether it is in catcalls at construction sites, the pressure of masculinity or the cookie cutter image of a beautiful wife. When sexism manifests in this way, it persists for everyone. This means that inequality is not a unique condition, neither is it out of the norm. This also means that the assumption that men and women are born equal is not necessarily true. Since gender-neutral language hoists this assumption, it undermines the conditions that gender differences create. In doing so, it does not adequately accommodate men or women and widens the gender differences. By this perspective, gender-neutral language renders legal frameworks counterproductive.

The argument against gender-neutral language is that true equality cannot be achieved unless unequal conditions are accounted and compensated for. The alternative, however, is developing gender-specific adaptations to legal frameworks.

Ironically, by prefacing said equality with preferential treatment, we're still treating men and women unequally.

Even if we can overlook the paradox, some would contend that this kind of equality is idealistic. The belief that men and women can be treated as entirely equal is illusive. Though it is possible, and essential, to develop legal frameworks that challenge sexism, the issue simply does not exist at an institutional level. It is not only about having fewer opportunities or access to education. It is also about the ideas that we've been brought up with - that women should not be heard, (and in some cases even seen!); that women's worth is tied to the kitchen; or that a woman must fit the pigeonhole of a 'perfect wife.' Without a change in these attitudes, there is little that gender-specific language can do. Rather, deviating from gender-neutral language may, in fact, reinforce the gender differences that ignite such attitudes and positions.

Language plays a critical role in the understanding of sexism and women's rights. While words have the power to dictate attitudes and treatment, they are also unwilling carriers of prejudice. The sheer magnanimity of language makes it complex to entirely favor gender equality, even with a conscious effort to do so.

"Human rights are women's rights, and women's rights are human rights."
– Hilary Clinton

5

Born This Way

*Biological differences in terms of feminism
and the argument against women's rights*

One of the key areas of contention in terms of women's rights is biological differences. When we talk about equal representation, it is argued that women and men are inherently (physically, biologically) different, so their rights can never be the same.

In today's world, worthy leaders don't necessarily have a nameplate that reads "mister" before their name. Worthy leaders, today, are smart, analytical and inventive. These traits do not come from biology. For one, many use biological differences to justify the wage gap. Despite the progression of women's rights, women all around the world are more likely to bear responsibility for the family, than men. Many argue that it is this dynamic which ties women to low-paying jobs offering the flexibility so essential to these 'necessary' responsibilities. This assumption puts forth the idea that men and women are endowed with different roles in society that directly follow their biological differences. This then becomes an explanation attached to the wage gap.

The argument that men and women are *meant* for different roles is unfounded. It is likely that women are associated with family and domestic responsibilities because of their biological capacity to bear children. However, this does not mean that biological differences make it such that women *should* be associated with family and domestic responsibilities. By allowing biological differences to determine gender roles, we simply reinforce social differences between men and women. In other words, men and women are not biologically *endowed* with different roles, but we allow biological differences to justify unequal roles. Accordingly, the concentration of women in low paying jobs is not the product of biological differences, but of a society that chooses to empower biology and, in the process, pressure women towards 'biologically relevant' social roles.

It is true that evolutionary psychologists have developed a strong case for this. They suggest that men and women have evolved differently and in turn carry psychological and physiological differences which play a role in behavior and capacity. Others argue that such differences stem from cultural and social dynamics, provoking a nature versus nurture argument. However, it is not necessary to reject the former on behalf of feminism.

People are likely to draw away from these ideas because they offer an unattractive image of human nature. Just because an explanation is unattractive does not mean it is false. Many proponents of gender equality find these explanations problematic. They believe that these explanations may take gender inequality as natural or inevitable and, in that process, even justified. This begs the question, do biological differences between men and women allow gender inequality to be made inevitable?

Evolution does not take place in consideration of morals; it merely bodies the movement and changes of humans, attributed to their genetic make-up. Evolutionary explanations do not dictate what is right or wrong, in the same way that the sole social impact of evolutionary phenomena is not necessarily right. Just because something is part of human nature does not necessarily mean it is something positive.

The way that men and women have evolved biologically may direct society towards male supremacy. This may illustrate a world where women are compliant to men and men command women only on the basis of brute strength and larger body structure afforded to men. However, accepting evolution as a factor that directs gender differences is not the same as accepting these gender differences.

In fact, supporting research in evolutionary theories or otherwise, may aid gender inequality. By uncovering the source of an unequal society, we are more likely to understand, and counter, those that act against women. Without being aware of what guides our behavior, we are less likely to change it.

Moreover, many supporters of gender equality that reject biological differences between men and women argue on the basis that inherent differences do not exist. Anatomical differences have been used many times to inflame gender roles and stereotypes. These differences do not point to one gender as better than the other. However, it is often interpreted in this way. As a result, those working for women's rights find themselves dismissing differences in biology.

At a time where science is at the forefront of all kinds of discourse, arguing against scientific evidence becomes counterproductive for the women's rights movement. This does not mean that it is necessary for all women's rights activists to believe in science; the movement is open to a host of different belief systems. However, by engaging in an anti-science discourse, we draw away from the real issues at hand and often welcome unnecessary criticism to the movement.

Dismissing biological differences as false stems from the assumption that women and men must be treated equally if they are equal in all other respects. It is often assumed that being biologically different makes women unworthy of being treated as equal to men. It also stands true for men who are forced into positions emotional strength socially because of their strength physically.

Stereotypes related to gender are often tied to biological differences. It is a concrete truth that men and women are biologically different. However, women are not biologically tied to white aprons, sandwich making skills and eye shadow in the same way that men are not biologically tied to grease, fist fights and six-pack abs.

In the process of misapplying stereotypes, we also perpetuate them. Since there is little that can dispute these biological differences, tying them to stereotypes means that there is little which can effectively counter these stereotypes. Ultimately, this approach further complicates the world's understanding and rejection of stereotypes, posing as a barrier for women's rights.

Though our world is polarized regarding the idea of disputing or accepting biological differences between men and women, it is the way that these differences are interpreted that impacts the women's rights movement.

There is no hormone that makes us less worthy of love and respect.

"Do not live someone else's life and someone else's idea of what womanhood is. Womanhood is you."

– Viola Davis

6

100% Human, Do Not Bleach

The Overlapping Struggle of Colorism and Sexism, and Unrealistic Expectations for Women

With 2016 marking the 15th year of the United Nations Durban Declaration against racism, the issues of colorism and prejudice once again saturated the social landscape. However, what was less confronted was their interloping role against women's rights.

It is clear that prejudice has a way of dehumanizing society. The harbinger of injustice, prejudice has a way of seeping callousness into the otherwise ordinary, warping the most familiar of events. We saw it in 20th-century propaganda machines, the theatrics of black faces and xenophobic plight – the images that we were both detached from and shackled to. When combined with an atmosphere of gender bias, it is haunting to see remnants of a blemished history take a stand in our present. Whether it is plastered across billboards or on the front cover of a magazine, colorism rallies gender stereotypes. Though this impact both men and women, it reinforces the stereotype of women as objects, based primarily on how they look.

In light of the world's eco-cultural metamorphosis, the relay to retail skin – bleaching products has dramatically escalated. Through the enrapturing rhetoric of cosmetic commercials, porcelain skin has been glorified, conveying a skewed standard of beauty. A concentrated picture is paraded as a generalized ideal. As beauty tethers itself to the grassroots of self-worth, the hue of one's skin becomes akin to demeanor. Since most of this is directed towards women, it validates those who argue that women are only worth their looks.

The objectification of women, when coupled with the pressure of reaching unrealistic standards, reinforces conformity. It inspires a mass-produced, cookie cut image and implies that all women should aspire for this image to be welcomed into society.

With this whitewashing leaking into the entertainment industry, the powers of digital editing and cosmetics have rendered dark skin obsolete. Appearances are misrepresented on behalf of vanity. In addition to this, the entertainment industry has long upheld the scaffolding of prejudice by parading behavioral stereotypes. In the absence of cross-cultural interactions, such polarized images have the ability to not only dictate attitudes towards certain groups, but also perpetuate generalizations.

In some parts of South East Asia, with matrimony domineering domestic scenarios, skin color becomes a factor when looking for the ideal partner. This sense of associating good companionship with light skin highlights how media-dictated standards prevail over perception and individual choice. Light skin, consequently, morphs into the hallmark of aristocracy, success and allure with the cosmetic industry serving as a vessel for such unrealistic ideals.

Tying into historical bias, this narrowing archetype forges the bedrock of color-hierarchy with "dark" flooding the bottom. While the cosmetic sphere's endorsement of light skin also undermines the idea of dark skin, economic parasitism breeds subconscious prejudice.

As this prejudice manifests into discrimination, the metaphysical gravities of colorism become a sobering reality. The spate of race-driven rampages has revealed the degree to which perceptions of color-based inferiority dominate evolving social dynamics. From the lynching of black immigrants to the harassment of women considered sub-desire merely because they don't bear a color aligned to the quintessential image, episodes of color driven violence have elucidated the dangerous personification of prejudice. The implications of these, however, bleed far from the social realm. By pouring into an atmosphere of product-perpetuated colorism, the surge of discriminatory brutality saddles a vibrant country like India with a melanin-void margin using dated attitudes as boulevards for repressed biases. In the context of impunity, it doesn't take much for isolated embers of hate crimes to ignite the roaring flame of collective acrimony. In lieu of penance, it appears as if holding stereotypes, or acting on prejudice, is a justified norm, part of the inalterable status quo.

This is, consequently, an issue detrimental to Indian society and it is our prerogative not to dispel blame at the abstract concept of colorism but at the concrete reality of individual choice.

*"I am not free while
any woman is unfree."*
– Audre Lorde

7

Trophy Wife
(Sister and Daughter)

Media Representation of
Women and its Role in Sexism

Media today plays a significant role in dictating how the world operates and what beliefs take form in society. Given the growth of women's rights movements, worldwide media has created a host of problems.

One of the most significant problems has been the representation of women in media. Whether in being treated as shallow, secondary characters, conforming to and perpetuating all gender stereotypes, developing storylines that victimize women or forcing an unrealistic beauty (and size) standard, the way that women are represented in media directs the approach towards women outside of media.

Many believe that it is impossible to stand against the scrutiny of the way the media portrays and represents women. Given the sheer magnitude and diversity of women worldwide, it is unrealistic to represent women accurately through a few contrived characters. It is also likely that women on television or in the theatre will be criticized at some level, regardless of what they portray. This reflects one of the principles directing much of the stigma against women: women are expected to be without character flaws, perfect from all points of view. Though the expectation to be perfect is also true for men, it is escalated further for women in the wake of existing gender inequality. It becomes almost counterproductive, because by pointing out character flaws in terms of being a "real woman," such critics dismiss acceptance for all women. By engaging in this kind of discourse, many of us increase the standards and expectations that already exist for women. In turn, many also argue that accurately representing the typical woman is impossible because there is no kind of woman that will be typical.

It is not surprising that many believe it is impossible to win. It is unrealistic to meet everyone's standards. Movies and television shows are developed with the objective of entertainment and profit. The belief that media is socially responsible for representing groups in an accurate way comes from viewers, not directors. In balancing these two objectives and an added social pressure, it is more likely, than not, that television shows and movies will not be able to achieve all three measures. It is also not surprising that they would choose their own objectives over the ones that are expected of them.

Many suggest that the expectation from the media is unsound. They argue that media exists for entertainment and should, accordingly, be separated from social movements. They imply that the media plays no role in modelling society, dismissing the dangers of misrepresentation. We cannot ignore the power that the media carries and the influence it has.

Even so, television and movies today often develop storylines that are realistic, imitating ordinary life and how many viewers live. The characters within these storylines also appear relatable, as if they could be part of our real lives. This means that most viewers would see characters in media as if they were ordinary, and if these characters either conform to or perpetuate stereotypes, then dated attitudes against women become normalized.

Social changes do not often translate to media. In spite of the immense progress that the world has made towards women's rights, women are still represented in the media in a 1950s image – subservient, helpless, perfect. Without being receptive to evolving norms, media often slows down the women's rights movement. It continues to undermine the progress by reflecting a dated version of social dynamics.

In some cases, television shows and movies carry a well-meaning, but misguided, approach to this problem with female characters that conform to the male stereotype. Though this attempts to empower women in the way that they are portrayed, some would argue that it positions femininity as weak. By implying that a female character is only strong or real if she acts like a man is supposed to, we unknowingly challenge the feminine.

Television shows and movies often cast actors who fit various beauty ideals for both men and women. However, bearing in mind that women are already treated in accordance to their appearance, this merely expands the expectation for women to look a certain way.

Take something as simple as the haircut of any actress worth her salt and recall how you have either wanted it for yourself or were asked to get your hair done like that.

In part, this divides the women's rights movement. By weighing one 'kind' of woman over another, media breeds unnecessary conflict. Though it might not always intend to, media places a women's worth as equal to the worth of her body, exploiting her appearance for 'entertainment.'

This kind of treatment applauds (or vilifies) women for a part of themselves that they have no control over. It also implies that women do not have depth, appearing secondary to their male counterparts.

Equally problematic are news reports that highlight gender over achievement. It is not uncommon to see headlines which read "female award winner" or "female truck driver." Though it is admirable that reports acknowledge the disadvantage that women are at and that they achieve while being on unequal footing, it is a problem when attention is drawn specifically to gender. In doing so, gender stereotypes are inadvertently reinforced by focusing on gender differences.

Though it is debatable whether media exerts a

positive or negative force towards the women's rights movement, it is clear that it has the potential to direct our thoughts towards or against gender roles and stereotypes.

"In the future, there will be no female leaders. There will be just leaders."

– Sheryl Sandberg

8

Second Place Feminist

Placing "right" and "wrong"
in social movements

One of the most significant myths circling is that feminists don't wear dresses. Well, if that's what it takes to be a feminist, then I don't think I'm a very good one. I like wearing high heels. I call my dad at first sight of a spider. I don't think I've lifted a hammer once in my life. I have to admit I liked watching Mad Men a lot more than I did Wonder Woman. My deviations from the rigid feminist are not as extravagant as most. What is more important is that they were choices I intentionally made. Some would perceive this as "bad" feminism, arguing that there can be a right and wrong in those that support social movements.

In the words of Roxane Gay, "The problem is not that she makes herself economically vulnerable in that choice; the problem is that our society is set up to make women economically vulnerable when they choose. Let's deal with that."

The difference lies in our interpretation of choices. Some find that feminists are those who choose to act against gender stereotypes, making a point to deviate from the behavior that is expected of them. They believe that a real feminist is one who does not act in line with what society perceives to be femininity. However, this also implies that women who do conform to these stereotypes or act in a way that can be construed as "feminine," are not feminists. Choosing to conform to the status quo does not mean that women want the status quo to remain as is. Beliefs do not often translate to action, but a lack of action should not automatically translate to a lack of belief. We assume that being a feminist is conditional on making choices that challenge stereotypes and femininity. However, it is also *the very act of exercising choice or of having the opportunity to choose that empowers women.* If a woman decides to stay at home and raise kids or take her husband's last name, she is not any less of a feminist than a woman who chooses the opposite. It is the ability and opportunity to make a choice that empowers the feminist movement.

Though this reasoning is sound, there are many groups that disagree with it. One could perceive conforming to stereotypes as reinforcing them. In this sense, their actions do nothing to help women's rights and may, in fact, complicate the case for these rights. Though we see silence as some neutral position, it is still a choice that can explain more than we think and making this choice determines the direction of our communication.

At the same time, it is hard to change what we don't recognize. If we avoid discussing our emotions or fostering a comfortable environment to do so, we do not subdue them. Rather, we betray coexistence. Since the feminist movement is already critiqued, viewing women's rights as a non-issue, many believe that women who conform to stereotypes reverse the progress the movement has made. In their view, being a feminist or even an activist rests on action, an active process to change the way things work right now.

In other words, it is widely debated whether

someone could believe in feminism without being an active feminist.

Ironically, this point of view undermines the disadvantages at which women are placed. Though many women may want to act outside of what is expected of them or deviate entirely from stereotypes, they may not be able to for fear of being isolated in society and family. Moreover, many women may hope for gender equality and women's rights, while not knowing what it takes to achieve these rights.

It also implies that women are only deserving of equal rights if they deviate from gender stereotypes, adding a kind of exclusivity to the outcomes of the feminist movement. However, this subverts the very principles on which feminism was formed. For one, feminism evolved with the goal of inclusivity in mind. By implying that some women are more deserving of human rights than other, we reverse years of progress. At the very basis of these movements is the idea that all women should be treated as equally as all men are.

Furthermore, if this pseudo-hierarchy remains, then it is likely to also occur in other areas of feminism. Proponents of this argument may suggest that women who are more disadvantaged deserve more rights than those who live comfortably. This blurs the lines between priority and unequal treatment. At the same time, in its scaffolding, feminism also carries the objective of acceptance and freedom.

With arguments like these which suggest that some women do not deserve feminism unless they make certain choices, we undermine a woman's freedom to make that choice. It also suggests that women who conform to stereotypes will not be accepted when, in fact, we are engaging in a battle with attitudes that don't accept women, period. There are some deviations from the rigid feminist image that are not as extravagant as most. Whether it is in liking pink, wearing dresses, allowing men to open doors or pay the check on a first date, listening to sexist music or reveling in media that objectifies women, there are many choices in everyday life that are seen as dictating where the feminist movement lies.

Many would contend that these are harmless. It would be misguided to direct resources and effort towards minor parts of everyday life when there are far more pervasive threats to women's rights such as access to education or availability of healthcare. Acting against these circumstances may place unnecessary problems for the industries from which they come. They may even go so far as to say that censoring pop culture is denying them the opportunity to express. It would be hypocritical to restrict women and men from the chance to express themselves, while advocating for freedom of choice. In this case, many see the need to separate media or entertainment from social causes. They argue that it is necessary because the objective of sexist music or movies that objectify women is not to fight for social causes, it is merely to entertain. By saying that the media is responsible for advocating for equal rights, we are placing a responsibility on them that they didn't sign up for.

Furthermore, by arguing that these should be censored, in the name of feminism, the movement is attracting unnecessary opposition from supporters of this kind of media. Considering that the support for feminism outside of feminists can be construed as bleak, we should be hesitant when garnering hostility among other groups. This may devolve the movement in a weaker position where it is further tied to an extremist subculture.

It is important to note that these minor choices in everyday life may be far more influential than we perceive them to be. By allowing for sexism to continue in the context of music or social norms, we implicitly allow for it to continue at a broader scale. Allowing these norms to continue may be seen as accepting them to be all right.

It is also likely that with the frequency of these norms, they are spread to a higher degree. Should teenage girls still nod in agreement because they *were* seen as the inferior sex? Should boys continue to bow to powers of chivalry, holding doors open and paying for bills in a world that otherwise propagates equality? "Courtesy" expects teenage boys to give up their seat for the comfort of women, asks teenage girls to set the table for dinner while men 'rest' from a whole day's work and infuses in tomorrow's world that they must – on behalf of politeness – put their own needs aside for both the strength and fragility of the opposite gender. Any deviations from the more "positive" strains of dated gender norms are, then, seen as unjustified rallies against basic courtesy.

However, in a world that leans towards equality, these attitudes are distant. The same decree carries for boys who hold the door open for themselves before they do for others. Their actions fall in line with the individualistic culture modern society upholds and demonstrates a measurable modern mindset. It is that idea of treating everyone as equal to us that exhibits courtesy – the idea that no one is superior or inferior to the respect you would request for yourself.

Nevertheless, our world still judges women for the choices they make. It may, however, seem misplaced to direct questions towards women who choose to act more "feminine" (in stereotype's terms) or brand them as "bad feminists." It is hypocritical to argue that certain choices make women less of a feminist. It seems to imply that there is a perfect kind of feminist that all women should aspire to.

This also dismisses the strength of ingrained gender roles or social conditioning. Though women and men may believe in gender equality and advocate for women's rights, it is difficult to counter years of believing in a norm. It is also difficult to recognize minor occurrences of sexism if we are led to believe that this is the way that things should work. Many also find that the status quo cannot be changed, as much as we may want it to.

Bearing this in mind, conforming to feminine stereotypes does not necessarily equate to being against feminism neither does it make someone a bad feminist. In spite of the considerations that need to be made to stand against sexist attitudes, it is as important to recognize these attitudes in the first place. Not doing so, indicates that a greater understanding of feminism is necessary.

*"All men should be feminists.
If men care about women's rights,
the world will be a better place.
We are better off when women are
empowered."*

– John Legend

9

Let Me Mansplain

Masculinity in the Context of Women's Rights

Ironically, one of the most pervasive dynamics of feminism and women's rights is masculinity. While the pressure for men to be more masculine is real, there is a double standard when it comes to masculinity. Many men are conditioned to behave towards women in a way that they would never behave towards men. Almost routinely, they subject women to a kind of treatment that would be unacceptable if directed towards other men. This isn't intentional: most men do not set out to parade male superiority in the face of disadvantaged women. It could be because (mis)education about masculinity, and the pressures to be masculine, perhaps rest on assumptions and stereotypes that men are strong, and women are weaker; men are superior, women inferior; women are meant to serve men in any way possible and women are to be owned by men, and so on.

The social pressure of acting masculine can make men less willing to support women's rights movements. Bearing in mind that women's rights place an emphasis on valuing femininity and accepting it in all its forms, it is not surprising that men who are pressurized to be 'masculine' would draw away from the movement. This sort of emphasis places men and women at opposite ends. It appears as if men *must* betray women's rights to maintain their masculinity and women *must* depart from men to maintain their own rights. In turn, the struggle of the women's rights movement is not merely against dated attitudes and institutions but also supporters who fear the implications of it in the modern-day world.

While it is true that women are penalized if they deviate from a perfectly crafted standard, men are also chastised for being unmanly.

It is a fact that many advertisements and

the media, in general, exploit masculinity. By portraying commercials that center on ruggedness or the "typical" stereotypes associated with men, they create a further divide between masculinity and women's rights. Since they emphasize strength as a male feature, they imply that women are weak. Moreover, it contributes to a culture that emphasizes the differences between men and women. It is important to note that such commercials reinforce the importance of masculinity, placing the image of a perfect man in tangent to one of a masculine man. This means that any man who chooses to challenge gender roles, for what is perceived as the less masculine approach, faces questions about his "manhood" and may, in turn, be less likely to support feminism.

It is also worthwhile to explore the many interpretations of masculinity and its role in sexism. Some argue that masculinity places heavy emphasis on strength, arguing that emotional or physical weakness has no part of the nature of men. It is therefore implied that if weakness is not natural to men, it must be natural to women. Brought forth in a daily scenario, this (mis)interpretation of masculinity would manifest as men not allowing their emotions to surface, such suppressed emotions turning into toxic behaviors, leading to atrocities on women, the perceived weaker gender.

While this insinuates femininity as being weaker than masculinity, it also makes it seem as if men and women embody certain, very different traits. While it is true that men and women are different, such a selective emphasis supports the argument that men and women contribute differently to society. If we accept that men and women are inherently different in skill or personality, we are also led to accept that the way in which they function in society must be different, supporting gender roles. When some of us do come to terms with this conclusion, we knowingly or unknowingly, justify why men and women are treated differently.

These paradigms also extend to the very concept of masculinity. The western media often romanticize the image of an 'assertive' man in tangent with the image of a 'model' man. From a psychological standpoint, this not only compels men to merge their identity with that of "machoism" and is likely to foster patriarchal mindsets. Joshua Goldstein argues that when gendered distinctions run this deep, they often seep into everyday practices – including domination in a gendered way.

It is also vital to discuss masculinity because it exposes the rigid definition of what it takes to be a man. Since men are expected to behave in a certain, masculine way, it would be unacceptable for women to behave in this same manner unless they would like to appear "manly." In doing so, the pressure of being masculine inclines men and women to dismiss changes in social expectations. Recognizing changes is a precursor to understanding them. Our differences are not only colossal; they are deep. Though we are a running spectrum of experiences, our true diversity is in thoughts. An open mind, I realized, is not limited to intellectual pursuits, but necessary to human relationships and the much-needed implementation of human rights.

In our world, we accept that sexism plays a significant role in society, at an institutional and personal level. The actions we take to address sexism are almost entirely directed towards women. Though it is true women are heavily disadvantaged, it is also important to note that the impact of sexism on masculinity and masculine culture is almost never discussed. Even without being discussed, the issue is pervasive in society. From an early age, boys are programmed with ideas about what it takes to 'be a man.' What makes it even more detrimental is that these messages are communicated subtly, hidden in norms and expectations, in toys and lessons, in ads on tv and dialogues at home.

The pressure of masculinity is not exclusive to an age or culture. In spite of a global move towards gender-neutral colors or toys, children are still conditioned to behave in a way that is "true" to their gender. Whether this is in the toxic belief that men don't cry, the idea that they must protect girls even if it puts them in danger. Boys are taught to stifle their humanity on behalf of masculinity. To express this strength, they are also taught to demean or victimize women.

Part of the problem lies in our culture. Masculinity demands that men resort to stoicism, repressing their emotions. Many men who perceive the expectations attached to masculinity have stalled their own ability to feel and communicate. Not only does this force emotional repression, but also implies that this kind of restraint is part of the culture and not the nature of men. Accordingly, women become convenient scapegoats for repressed frustrations and dated attitudes, while many of those raised in this environment lack the empathy that is needed for the women's rights movement to survive.

One of the hallmarks of women's rights or

gender equality movements is that they are effective because they are united. With this emphasis on fighting battles on your own and acting as an individual, men are less inclined to join a movement that requires a united front. Accordingly, it has become conventional to bear a nature that is self-serving rather than self-effacing. This system weighs on personal freedom and liberty, essentially giving individuals the means to thrive under the umbrella of universal values. Sometimes, the pursuit for individual agendas lies at the bedrock of social inequality. Without the guaranteed benefit posed by group success, individuals become incongruent in their ability to achieve and prosper. This separates the ties of society that make coexistence possible, thereby undermining the importance of feminism as a collective movement.

Many, however, perceive the concept of masculinity as harmless. The idea that masculine traits are stronger or better than feminine ones is purely a social construct. While masculinity is traditionally associated with action, courage and competition, femininity is associated with compassion, intuition and sympathy. However, we are sold on the fiction that a compassionate and intuitive person is somehow weaker than one that is competitive and active.

Criticism of masculinity often stems from proponents of women's rights; they also make it seem as if women's rights cannot exist with masculinity and that masculinity cannot exist without fracturing women's rights. Therefore, men who would like to support feminism are made to choose between their personal assimilation with society and that of the other gender.

If we consider sexism in the context of our world today, it is still associated solely with women and the struggles they have to endure. When sexism is discussed, it primarily references women. In a way, this is a good thing which shows that the battle for women's rights is still at the forefront of our social landscape. Since many would perceive women as being at a more significant disadvantage than men, it is understandable for the world to emphasize women's issues. This does draw away from men's issues. We are led to believe that struggles faced by men or biases pushed toward them are not part of sexism. It illustrates the myth that the sexism movement can direct focus only towards women or men when in fact the nature of the movement is to address all problems of equality.

In this way, masculinity stands at the forefront

of the women's rights movements. The way that masculinity is perceived and exercised impacts gender equality.

*"When men are oppressed,
it's a tragedy.
When women are oppressed,
it's tradition."*

– Letty Cottin Pogrebin

10

How Many Women Does It Take to Get a Joke?

The Problems and Defense with Sexist Humor

Can you laugh at a sexist joke without being sexist? Does sharing a sexist joke inflate prejudice? Are we supposed to abhor sexist jokes? Why do women laugh at misogynistic jokes? Why, in a world where #MeToo is necessary, are we drawn to this kind of entertainment?

The characteristics of humor do not allow for these answers to be as simple as we would like them to be. Humor is not only necessary; it is also powerful. Whether it is in the expansive field of political discussion, the ability to spotlight social injustice and hypocrisy or mirror the innate absurdity of our lives, humor is an essential part of the world. It has the power to engage an audience, draw it in and ask it to listen. Humor allows us to ask essential questions, push us to think and shape how we perceive the present to help us shape the future.

As crucial as humor is, it carries an emphasis on the same gender differences that mar pop culture. It would be misguided to suggest that all humor is powerful or that all humor has a purpose. Some humor might exist purely to laugh or generate laughs. Humor is difficult to separate from gender and leads us to ask what is the cost of generating a laugh? Are sexist jokes as 'powerful' or 'necessary' as the ones that infiltrate political discourse? Or are they as harmless as the ones which exist just for getting a laugh?

Siyanda Mohutsiwa once posed an interesting explanation for why women, knowing the bias perpetuated, participate in this kind of humor. She argues that it is a mechanism of our political and social atmosphere, a world where women are treated as second to men. From singing along with sexist rap music to enduring commercials that objectify women, to laughing at a sexist joke, it can be refreshing to inflict gender biases instead of receiving them. "Taking back" these jokes gives women the means to escape their own vulnerability, granting them a kind of power where they are not unwilling victims of sexism but willing participants in it.

Others would say that they participate because it is harmless. We often hear "overreaction" in synonym with "feminism." It is, therefore, the ability to speak against the status quo that challenges not simply sexist rhetoric but also demonstrates the outrage for a movement that is, at its root, a plea for equality. They would say that in nitpicking or dissecting the minutest parts of society, we embody the same stereotypes which brand feminists as extremists. In fact, this may increase hostility against women's rights movements. More often than not, it is those unaffected by misogyny that sustain misogynistic humor. If they are "attacked" or questioned by feminists, they may be less willing to join and understand women's rights movements. Objecting to sexist humor asks for a change, albeit small, in the way that men and women interact. However, it is human nature to draw away from change and asking for change using humor could foster an aversion against the people asking for this change. Rather than directing resources towards minor barriers to gender equality, it may be more worthwhile to challenge the real proponents of sexism.

The assumption that sexist humor is merely a minor barrier or that it doesn't demand a serious reaction is not true. In the wake of the stereotypes that persist with a polarized image of women, this kind of humor deepens the prejudice against women. As far as we find ourselves propelled into the advent of the digital era, there remains an inherent part of us shackled to primitive instincts. Because of this we often use first impressions and stereotypes in how we behave and speak. Since this kind of humor reinforces these stereotypes, they become part of our subconscious.

The most lethal part of prejudice is when the bias we possess seeps into our subconscious. Since it is difficult to identify, the very concept of hidden behavioral influences makes subconscious prejudice very difficult to change. No moral person believes that race is enough reason for hate, that mere gender can be reason to restrain abiding members of society. However, as the conscious draws towards logic and reason, it is our subconscious that hauls the other way. This, many would perceive, is the product of small, 'harmless' parts of society.

In the context of our society, the prejudice against women is ancient. The subtler – and arguably less harmful - influences of misogyny leak into daily life. Whether this is the thinly veiled suggestions to behave more 'lady-like,' wear only certain types of clothes, the perception of women as just a means for reproduction or even the unrealistic expectations of women, society becomes blind to such undercurrents.

Subconscious prejudice does not merely exist but is a springboard from which damaging behaviors emerge. To combat these issues, it is necessary to become a force conducive to the demise of gender discrimination. What remains, in this sense, critical is coloring the rather invisible process of sexism.

The problem is that sexist humor is neither benign nor harmless. These kinds of jokes allow many to express sexism and biases against women comfortably. This, in turn, impacts the way men and women perceive social rights and wrongs. More importantly, sexist jokes act as vehicles for sexist sentiments while also perpetuating sexism amongst those that condone it. In this process, women and men are led to believe that sexist jokes are socially acceptable and, by extension, so is the sexism it entails.

This is especially true when we consider jokes that make light of serious problems like sexual harassment. By making it acceptable to joke about sexual harassment, we normalize it. This normalization desensitizes men and women from these issues, associating these subjects with humor rather than the detrimental impacts they have in real life. To foster an atmosphere that is equal and safe, we have to channel equality at every level, even when it comes to humor.

So, though some would perceive sexist humor as harmless and action which abhors such jokes as unnecessary, there is a sound argument against this kind of entertainment.

"Feet, what do I need you for when I have wings to fly?"

– Frida Kahlo

One Size Fits All?

*Feminism and Overlapping
Social Contexts*

In today's world, many find that women's rights movements face the threat of being branded as irrelevant. All feminists are not heterosexual, white and financially able.

Intersectionality is the perspective that women are attacked with prejudice and bias in a host of different ways, varying in the extent of depth and kind of struggle. This suggests that gender-based prejudice does not merely change in light of social contexts but is also heavily guided by "intersectional systems of society." Whether it is in terms of social class, appearance, race or sexuality, women experience oppression differently dependent on the context that they are in.

Intersectionality in women's rights movements can also be explained through the many layers and facets of a profile. In other words, different women face different struggles and are oppressed in different ways. While sexism is a key player in an unequal world, it cannot be isolated from the equally weighed issues of racism, ageism, classism and other matters. It is difficult to conceive a one size fits all approach towards feminism or a single kind of feminist.

However, as important as intersectionality has been to the feminist movement over many years, its understanding has only become widespread recently. This leaves many men and women unaware of what intersectionality means to a feminist and how much weight it carries when considering approaches towards women's rights, breeding greater divisions within the feminist movement.

In many ways, intersectional feminism is perceived as a clear path towards harmony, sowing hope for racial unity and integration of cultures.

As logical as intersectionality in feminism is in theory, there is a pool of problems that appear when it is exercised. Caucasian women hold significant racial advantages given the different histories of prejudice and bias. Though they may join in the understanding of intersectional feminism, it is difficult to understand the struggles of a racial disadvantage if they haven't been experienced. Intentionally or not, many Caucasian women who identify themselves as intersectional feminists are separated from the problems faced by women who are of a different race and may find it difficult to truly understand these problems. This undermines the unity and understanding that intersectional feminism asks for. At the same time, women who face racial discrimination or biases are detached from intersectionality in feminism as well. Due to these experiences with racial hostility or cultures of indifference, some of these women are less likely to sympathize with those whom they perceive as being more privileged. This, inadvertently, divides the feminist movement to a greater extent, fostering competition between races.

While intersectional feminism may include multiple kinds of social contexts, greater emphasis is placed on the problems associated with race. An assumption that follows is that all Caucasian women are privileged, dismissing the overlapping facets of class or sexuality. This further breeds animosity and division in the feminist movement, distracting from the goal of bringing equality between men and women.

If feminism is seen as a movement for equality between men and women, achieved through women's rights, intersectionality in feminism is the view that overlapping characteristics are important and that factors like race, class, sexuality, religion or ethnicity can influence the way in which different women experience life.

Intersectionality in feminism is especially necessary in today's world as we confront a kind of reality that leaves women vulnerable in many ways. It is clear that we are lengths away from the equality we've been promised and the equality we deserve. Women in all parts of this world have to choose to exercise the rights that they have by virtue of being human and are put in danger because of it. It is easy to ignore these issues because we don't consider the progress that has been made. As these attitudes surface with greater ferocity than before, the rights we have already secured are also at threat. Feminism, today, falls to the problem of misinterpretation with intersectionality. Women face the significant danger of feminism being treated as an exclusive movement. Many women find that feminism can exist exclusively and operate by excluding those with fewer privileges and fewer opportunities to exercise their voice. These are the very people that require feminism. Without understanding the many angles of privilege and social contexts, it is difficult to ensure that all women are treated in the same manner.

Many would argue that intersectionality is both misunderstood and misused. The definitions that surround intersectionality are very diverse and rarely agreed upon.

A paradox unfolds when we consider intertextuality in terms of feminism. While it is the nature of feminism to remain united and treat women equally, it is in the nature of intersectional feminism to stand by our differences. We must honor our differences while maintaining our advocacy.

"...her wings are cut and then she is blamed for not knowing how to fly."

– Simone de Beauvoir

Yes, But Not Like That

Double Standards Between Men and Women, and Expressions of Uneven Footing

Regardless of how progressive their world is, women and men are subject to massive double standards. While they are expected to act one way, they are in conflict with countless social laws and expectations. In the process, of abiding by all of these demands, we often lose sight of what it takes to live in an equal world.

These double standards are reflected in the greatest literary works. Though few of us would ascertain parallels between Greek literature and 21st-century reality, gender roles in Homer's epic poem, The Odyssey, express the same double standards that hold true for our reality today. In the Odyssey, Odysseus, the (male) hero, takes part in a journey home after fighting in the battle of Troy. While voyaging back to his home, Ithaca, Odysseus disregards his marriage by spending eight years with Calypso and Circe, two women that are characterized simply by their good looks. As a man, his infidelity is interpreted as entirely conventional, and necessary to have the rest of his crew freed from Circe's grasp. Women, however, are expected to remain loyal, rather than have multiple sexual partners acceptable for men. This is particularly evident when Odysseus' wife, Penelope, is illustrated as "far too prudent" to be unfaithful. She is held at expectations far different than those set out for men, and while she is complimented for being prudent, the flattery comes at the expense of placing her at an unequal footing when compared with Odysseus.

Women are also penalized if they deviate from a perfectly crafted standard. After understanding that some of Odysseus' maids slept with the suitors, he put them to death for exemplifying the same sexual promiscuity and lack of loyalty considered customary for men. By displaying acceptance of behavior when conducted by men while condemning it if done by women, the poem unveils the double standards for fidelity between men and women.

As the poem takes its course, a variety of Odysseus' obstacles are resolved through infidelity. Had Odysseus had remained faithful, being held to the same standard that is expected of women, and not slept with Circe, his crew might have been trapped on Circe's island for eternity. A simple act of remaining loyal would fracture the entire plot of the poem by causing an inescapable block. Unwittingly, this portrays disloyalty as a necessity for men rather than a misdemeanor, as with women.

These double standards further reveal a difference in male and female social power that is increasingly relevant today. Interestingly, women in this poem are provided with an almost great extent of social influence. However, this influence is often overpowered by the men's superior social power. For instance, Penelope is able to influence her community into believing and her serving women into hiding the loom she wove for her father-in-law. This influence, however, eventually runs out causing the serving women to reveal the truth, thereby encouraging her family to force a remarriage upon her.

On the other hand, Odysseus is able to influence and convince several individuals to hide his true identity, when he returns to Ithaca, without any similar consequences. One of the main factors that contribute to women's social power in this epic is their resort to temptation. For example, Circe's lure entices Odysseus and his comrades to spend an entire year away from their journey home, accompanying her on her island. However, Circe's social influence is overpowered by Odysseus power and authority as a man, in directing the crew back home.

This is incredibly relevant to our world today where women are still held at a separate standard than their male counterparts. At the same time, these women are denied a voice and their actions overridden by men.

Kate Chopin is renowned for writing about women that transcend the norm. She has developed a framework of literature that questions society. This is particularly true for her use of indirection in the short story, "The Kiss." By obscuring the lines of her narrative, Chopin implies that underneath social conventions, a diverse reality exists.

In one story, Nathalie finds herself in a love triangle where she is engaged to Brantain but might still have a connection with another man, Harvy. Nathalie's dynamic with Brantain mirrors a life of social convention

– the concealment of which speaks to an incompatibility with limits. Chopin draws upon the idea of incompatibility with Brantain. She also argues that Nathalie is incompatible with the demands of society that Brantain mirrors. Moreover, Chopin's choice to withhold insight into Brantain's character makes him appear unfitting to the storyline. He appears as a secondary challenge to the passionate discourse between Harvy and Nathalie. This disconnects Brantain, not simply from the narrative, but also from Nathalie herself – making him seem like an incompatible match to her personality. As Brantain falls into the mold of a socially conforming man, he becomes a metaphor for the cultural limits imposed upon women at the time. Therefore, his relationship with Nathalie becomes a mirror for the conflict between how women are and how they are expected to be. In the wake of this theme, the narrative gaps speak of how Nathalie, much like other women at the time, is incompatible with the stereotypical told of femininity. Nathalie mirrors the difficulty of conforming to the definition of 19th-century femininity. This circles back to Chopin's idea of there being more to the world than our status quo may suggest. Through this, Chopin comments on the rigidity of social constructs – reinforcing the ends that women have to go to when their desires conflict with the image they are forced to uphold.

The duality of Nathalie's life symbolizes the much broader landscape of women and expectations of society. From a broader perspective, Chopin chooses to conceal insight into her characters. Rather, she draws them as silhouettes – basing their characterization purely at the surface. While this appears generic, it also positions the characters as a representation of society as a whole. Therefore, Nathalie's struggle to balance the curbed image expected of her and her true "outspoken" personality mirrors the confined condition forced upon women at the time. Her choice of indirection becomes an intricate comment on the injustice in her society and a symbol for things demanding change.

Both of these literary works mirror a reality which continues to hold true for our world today. They were written in the context of the distant past. While Homer's Odyssey mirrors the gendered realities of ancient Greece, Chopin's short story reflects the heavy and rigid standards placed on women in the 19th century, both of which apply to the details of sexism in 2018, a world that is supposed to be very different from those of the past.

This truth is sobering.

These double standards exist because of the progress that women's rights have made. The growth of feminism and the increase of women's rights movements has made it possible for women to have more opportunities today than they ever had in the past. Though many still perceive women to be inferior, there are many parts of this world that open education, career and family doors for women regardless of who they are. Ironically, the results have not been entirely positive. The progress in women's rights and the open-minded changes are matched with those who remain close-minded, choosing to use this progress to constrain women even further. Knowingly or not, many men and women now increase the expectations they place on women.

It is demanded that women still conform to what is conventionally expected of them in addition to the expectation of breaking stereotypes and succeeding more than men. Our world insists on fracturing any hope of a progressive, freer tomorrow because it continues to place harsh standards on women. What is even worse is that women are judged from all ends, but not just by men. The harshest critics are more often than not, other women.

Though the world has made enormous strides to secure women's rights and gender equality, we continue to perceive positions of authority as roles that are traditionally handed off to men. At the same time, we perceive women to be wavering in these roles, while expecting them to challenge the status quo, taking on traditional authority positions without succumbing to gender customs. More often than not, when they do take on these roles, they are seen as women taking on a man's job. This can also appear almost positive. When we congratulate women on breaking the glass ceiling and taking on 'a man's role,' we are still acknowledging that it is, indeed, a man's role. As such, the women that take on positions, of authority or otherwise, that are traditionally associated with men continue to be perceived as exceptions, rather than the norm. When women accept these positions, they are also expected to behave in a certain way. 'The man's way.' They are reminded to keep their femininity in check. Women are expected to carry traditionally feminine roles because when they assume traditionally male roles, they are seen as women taking on *men's* positions rather than women taking on *new* positions. This is a double standard. Even when women break the constraints that are imposed upon them, they are constantly reminded of their primary duty. Whether it is to balance family with work, cater to their partner's newly found emasculation, maintaining a position of submission despite being the breadwinner or working twice as hard for half as much, women everywhere are subject to double standards that challenge any movements towards equality. A great example of this is seen in an interview with the chief executive of a large food and beverages company who says that her mother reminds her to leave her position outside the door when she enters back home. There, she is reminded, she is still mother, wife and daughter!

It would, however, be unfair to perceive double standards concerning women without considering the repercussions on men. Women's rights movements around the world place special emphasis on choice, to stay at home and raise children, to pursue a professional life at the expense of traditional female roles or to ignore the "rules" society has set out for us. We argue for the ability to make a choice, implying that it is a necessary part of being human. We also put forth the idea that it is the ability to exercise choice rather than what we choose which should be under the spotlight.

Men also face considerable judgment when they choose; it is simply less common and less prevalent than it is for women. A man who chooses to stay at home is often perceived as less able than a man who chooses the opposite. At the same time, the women's rights movement, and many social movements, around the world place increasing importance on the value of expression and emotion. Men are still chastised for expressing any feelings because it would stand as an impediment to their strength. This follows the unwavering expectation that they must always remain strong.

The implications posed are serious, not only for the men that have to navigate through these double standards but also for women. If we continue to expect men to embody the values opposite of those that we fight for, we perpetuate masculine gender roles. If gender roles exist of men, then any action out of the bounds of what is traditionally perceived as female will still be considered a man's way.

At the forefront of any social change stand conflicting standards, blocking any step for progress and sending us back to the start line.

"Don't let anyone tell you you're weak because you're a woman."

– Mary Kom

From Beauvoir to Hashtags

The evolution of women's rights protests and their part in a changing world

Many would argue that, over the years, the nature of women's rights protests has remained the same: it is a parade of thoughts and ideas that all advocate for gender equality. While this may hold true, it is equally clear that the method for parading these thoughts and ideas has changed over time. Many of the messages protested in the past are relevant to our present, but it is only through a progression of communication that these messages have continued to be useful in the way that they illustrate the importance of women's rights.

Jeremy Popkin attributes the growing discontent
with the status quo to "long-term trends,"
specifically the growth of public opinion
and enlightened thought. Though he writes
about the French revolution in its entirety, his
words apply to the splintered women's rights
movement that captivated much of Europe at
the time and flourished alongside the battle for
democracy. In line with this, Popkin aligns the
"influence" of the Enlightenment to breeding a
major social and political revolution. Criticism
of institutions among rising philosophers
cultivated revolutionary sentiments within the
public. This kind of thought dominated France,
in particular, by developing concepts of justice
and emphasizing how the king's reign stunted
them. It was through the long-term trend of
Enlightenment that the idea of a revolution
emerged. While this stood primarily concerning
the monarchy, it also played a role in women's
rights. Enlightenment also gave rise to the
long-term trend of growing public opinion and
interest. With emerging beliefs, many women
began to consider the hypocrisy in the political
revolution: they were fighting for human rights
and freedom while accepting the constraints
they face at home, tied to the kitchen.

One of the earliest forms of women's
rights protest emerged in the form of Mary

Wollstonecraft, Olympe de Gouges and Judith Sargent Murray. They rose as prominent advocates of women's rights and championed the heart of equality within sexes. This advocacy emerged in strong form in the 1790s as a result of Enlightenment thought and the prejudice enveloping key ideas at that time. The Age of Enlightenment was a product of European philosophers, characterized by dramatic shifts in the paradigms of philosophy and politics as nuanced thinking was emphasized. While this triggered the French revolution itself, it also sparked the ideas of human rights and universal education. With this, the women's rights movement was born.

In 1791, Olympe de Gouges published *The Declaration of Rights of Woman and Citizen.* Modeled along the same language as its forbearing document, de Gouges – to some degree – mocked their gender bias and instead advocated for women's rights. Her response not only fostered the gender equality movement, but it also sparked a series of advances in women's rights advocacy.

In *A Vindication of the Rights of Woman,* Mary Wollstonecraft wrote of the importance of reason and, by extension, universal education. Although Wollstonecraft contended that women should continue retaining their traditional role in domestic life, she also believed that universal education could further advancement in society – well in line with the principles of the enlightenment. For the most part, Wollstonecraft attributes the ascendancy of mankind to the concepts of virtue, reason and knowledge. Considering the power of virtue, she claims that women without education aren't aware that they "ought to be virtuous." Consequently, they raise a generation unconcerned with the importance of "moral(s)" and the "civil interest" of humanity. Ultimately this hinders the development of an intellectual society and instead promotes individual and insignificant pursuits. Accordingly, she implies that the progress of a nation is dependent on how educated women foster reasons, virtue and knowledge in the future society.

Her thoughts almost wholly aligned with Judith Sargent Murray. In *On the Equality of Sexes,* Sargent Murray argued that the deficit between males and females results not from inferiority of the female sex, but from a difference in opportunity. Murray argues that gender inequality stems from a "difference of education." She also contends that reason is considered as a justification for male superiority. However, this reason is molded from the knowledge that is denied to the female population. Therefore, lack of reason cannot be attributed to the "inferiority of (the female) sex" but to the denial of information that snatches ability from the female mind. As a result, without education, women, unable to exercise their intellectual curiosity, shift their focus to the trivial concerns of "scandal" – withholding the betterment of society.

Furthermore, she notes that while men are continually taken down the path of science, women are "wholly domesticated." In particular, her diction implies that when lacking education, women are tethered to the household and led by the 'superior' sex. Wollstonecraft and Murray's ideas fall in line with Enlightenment thought that challenged traditionalism in exchange for advances to society. Subsequently, education is an important theme in women's rights because it enables women to acquire the very traits that elevate male superiority.

By advocating for this right, Olympe de Gouge also spoke of a woman's right to "freely" discuss the "paternity" of her child. Consequently, she implied that children born out of wedlock are equal to those born in legitimate marriages. Her assertion greatly challenged the existing belief that only males had to right to exercise their sexuality outside of marriage, without consequent responsibilities.

Furthermore, by attributing a child's recognition to "their fathers" as well, de Gouge questioned the prospect of women being the sole instruments of reproduction. This instigated that the role of males surpassed politics and rationality but also extended to reproduction – a sphere exclusively pertaining to women at the time. Subsequently, if men could hold a role in the traditionally female realm of society, women could too assume positions in the political society. This dynamic and this kind of footing stands true even in 2018.

Women like Wollstonecraft and Murray were not considered complete citizens in the time that they were in and, therefore, did not assume the freedom of speech. Their voices and their writing acted as a sign of protest. At a time where their world was placing greater importance on thought and writing, they positioned themselves as participants in a collective movement for human rights, making it clear that women's rights are a part of human rights.

Having said that, what these women do best is illustrate a need for feminism that applies to the 21st century. Though their words were written in revolutionary France, the principles that they argue for still stand true today and are essential to view in light of current feminist dynamics.

However, as much as these ideas apply to today's world, this kind of activism would not work today.

The pace at which technology is growing makes it easier for the written word to be distributed and growing networks in a globalized world subvert the barriers of language. At the same time, there has been an increasing appreciation for the freedom of speech as countries around the world begin to place a greater emphasis on democratic values. These trends combine to make a clear case for the importance and effectiveness of the written word in our world today.

It also undermines the extent to which this importance and effectiveness are exercised. It is now becoming more convenient to publish, post or share the written word than it was in the past, there is also an increase in the amount of written word that is published, posted or shared. Bearing in mind that the women's rights movement is as pervasive as it is, the amount of un-vetted written thoughts on feminism escalates by the minute. Even if the 21st century Wollstonecraft, Murray or de Gouges were to write about the struggles of a modern woman, it is unlikely that they would receive the attention they deserve. Our world has made it such that enrapturing thoughts are broken down to buzzwords and hashtags. It would not be surprising if a written protest is overlooked, neither would it be surprising if this protest is eclipsed by more trivial tweets, vines or snaps. Thus, one of the most apparent ways in which protest can effectively take place today is through these same tweets, vines or snaps.

A more recent avenue where this takes form is the repurposing of late night comedy. While late night comedy shows are popularly branded as a convenient and entertaining source of information, many find that it is an ineffective form of protest, misinforming the public with clouded opinions. However, it is misleading to argue that late-night comedy only leads the audience towards conservative political and social views; if viewed in the context of liberalism, late-night comedy effectively contributes to a well-informed public. From the liberal perspective, humans are inherently self-seeking and incentivized to increase their understanding of social development. Since late-night comedy carries the dual purpose of entertainment and communication, they underscore vital points while detracting from background details. In this dynamic, the "self-seeking" nature of humans translates to increased viewer interest in sociopolitical content. In turn, these viewers are more likely to read conventional news to find context for satirist monologues. In terms of global politics, a well-informed public is far from "devastating" to political discourse. Instead, it offers models for an exchange of ideas which ultimately challenges social norms.

This becomes particularly important in terms of feminism and women's rights. By contributing to a world that is better informed and more aware of women's rights violations, this kind of narrative directs the audience towards greater sensitivity when it comes to women's rights and equality. Though this works positively, by creating a world that better understands what it takes to progress, some may also point out that this is dangerous.

Many people acquire all of their information solely through late-night comedy. While they protest the problems in society through satire and humor, the producers, directors and actors of these late-night comedies are also thrust with the responsibility to inform with accuracy. By ceding all authority to one source, we fall to misunderstanding. What we accept as fact is often open to questioning. The truth relies on perspective, and it is rare to find them separated. As such, the narratives that we take as fact may be far more contrived than we initially assume. Our current sources of information do not carry complete details. Rather, they are partial stories; they build a foundation that precedes our own construction of knowledge. If these shows chose to draw away from women's rights issues and focus on other ones, it is likely that viewers will also begin to treat women's rights issues with less importance. In other words, if it is not worthy of screen time, then it is likely not very important. While this is the assumption that most viewers have, it is not true. A trend does not make an issue important or relevant.

Nevertheless, this could be an exaggeration. If late-night comedy and talk shows can direct viewers towards better recognizing the problems in our socio-political landscape, particularly women's rights, they can also transpire their media-based protest into something that is even more concrete. By sensitizing the world to these issues, they are likely to spark even greater movements for change.

This is particularly effective in today's world where many people find it difficult to trust the news. Because we live in a world where "fake news" and "alternative facts" not only exist but are also normalized, men and women everywhere do not trust information about women's rights that is spurred through conventional news sources. What late night comedians do is that they make their position clear. They do not hide their opinions behind a veil of what is called, but not widely perceived as, objectivity. Moreover, they put a face in front of the information that is being rallied, leading the audience towards believing that they are more trustworthy than the sources they are used to. This means that regardless of what they convey, late-night comedy is listened to, to a higher degree than other kinds of news. However, what they express is often in support of human rights, particularly gender equality and they do so in a way that questions the status quo. Moreover, in doing so, they foster a new form of protest that has become increasingly effective

This kind of trend also stands true for protest through social media. Twitter, in particular, has unveiled an interesting dichotomy between modern and pre-21st-century political activism. Let's take a walk back in time to 1934, to the Jarrow Crusade of England. Visualize one of the most important protests of English history being carried out by close to two hundred men, men who have been recruited through days of publicizing in spoken word or printed text. Picture marching for a petition to re-establish the town's industry, and consequently, challenge severe unemployment; yet, see the community fall short of any immediate action in the Parliament. Now, visualize Cairo in 2011. See the epicenter of another pressing protest. Envision three hundred thousand protesters willfully demonstrating against their government and the method of governance. However, rather than the spoken word, we see that the majority of recruitment happen through the press of a button, a few hashtags and a hundred and forty characters or less. These results, in today's world, are hard to achieve with the simplicity of spoken word and printed text. Such kind of media is a thread of international communication that stitches itself into the fabric of such activism. The prospect of expressing your ideas to an extensive online community has dramatically shaped society's ability to spread and write concepts politically or otherwise without restrictions.

The primary bane with such an open platform is that it often gives way for radicals promoting false facts. Although feminists around the globe differ slightly in intentions - as a consequence of culture or upbringing - historians and archives assert that the true intention is universal gender equality. Yet, in the early stages of this movement, Twitter - and all social media alike - were heartily embraced by extremists parading the negative notion of feminine superiority. While opinion is more than valued, many believe Twitter provides an outlet to cloud dictionary defined facts with radical perceptions.

Nevertheless, it has allowed for more concrete action to be better known. If we consider the "#MeToo" movement, this becomes clearer. Though the "MeToo" movement started as a message for support towards victims of sexual harassment in the Hollywood Film industry, the use of a hashtag - #MeToo - allowed it to transform into a sign of protest against years of male dominance and the loss of the female voice. Because the hashtag is such an easy vehicle to spread information quickly, when attached to women's rights messages, it can transform ideas into movements.

In this way, women have been able to unite their messages of protest under a virtual umbrella, contributing to a collective protest against years of unfair treatment.

From Cleopatra, the ancient Egyptian queen and the nation's final pharaoh, who defended Egypt against the Roman Empire and spoke nine languages to the Suffragettes (Mary Wollstonecraft, Susan B. Anthony, Alice Stone Blackwell, Elizabeth Cady Stanton,

Emmeline Pankhurst, Sojourner Truth) who in the first major rallying cry for feminism, fought vehemently for women's rights, most specifically, the right to vote. From Simone de Beauvoir, social activist, social theorist, and author of *The Second Sex*, an ahead-of-its-time book credited with paving the way for modern feminism to Alice Paul. From Eleanor Roosevelt – the first First Lady to speak out for women's rights to Betty Friedan who is credited to have started the second wave of feminism through her The Feminine Mystique to Gloria Steinmen, fondly referred to as the Mother of Feminism, to Frida Kahlo to Oprah Winfrey to Emma Watson to Malala Yousafzai to Priyanka Chopra, history and modern times are replete with women who continue to focus their lives on the empowerment, freedom and emancipation of women around the world.

Each feminist in their own right has done what it takes to build, educate about and reform the potent movement that is feminism.

Feminism, however, as beset by its own issues as discussed throughout the essays, needs more people to understand it for what it truly is and then take up the cause.

Can we really afford to have, what ideally should be, 50% of the world's population feel oppressed, suppressed and be depressed because of it?

Can we really allow for the other 50% to bear the brunt and pressures of society even if they don't want to, even if they feel differently?

What bears deep thought from people with power, and without, is the impact of a failed feminist movement in times to come.

As we gear for a new wave of feminism, to make for a better, more balanced world, each one of us looking at our values, beliefs and unconscious biases about feminism becomes of utmost importance.

I hope we all do so.

I hope you look at your own understanding of, and involvement in, feminism today.

Acknowledgements

My parents, without whom nothing would be possible. Thank you for everything. I wouldn't be the person that I am, if it wasn't for you.

Ms. Catherine Geisen-Kisch, who always has her door (and heart) open - no matter how many times I drop by her office. Thank you for believing in me.

Mr. Lyle Greer, Mr. Lukas Gohl and Ms. Rucha Bhayani – you inspire me everyday. I am incredibly lucky to have learnt from you.

Dr. Lina Kim, a woman I am so incredibly grateful to know and have learnt from. Lina, you have shown me that our voices can reach far and our compassion matters. Every time I have had the opportunity to speak with you, I am inspired, supported and thankful.

Ms. Ulka Adivrekar and Ms. Crystal Van Cleef, for showing me constant love and support. I am so thankful for everything you have done for me and taught me.

Gokha Amin Alshaif, for demonstrating what it takes to be strong and true to who you are. Thank you for the endless support and care.

Zach Rentz, for making me look forward to 8 AM lectures with a world of guidance and encouragement. Thank you so much for everything.

My friends, the world's greatest lady Supremes, midnight pancake professionals, dry lab family, quarterback, big sister and honey emoji.

About the Author

Vedika Kanchan is a grade 12 student at the Oberoi International School. In addition to all her extracurricular pursuits, she also excels at academia. A year ago, she took her IGCSE final exams and received the Oberoi International School Merit Scholarship, which carries a significant tuition waiver for both junior and senior year. She has also taken honours English courses at Stanford University's Online High School.

Vedika has been a writer for as long as she can remember. In addition to having 11 articles published in a national newspaper (DNA), she has also contributed to student publications in Stanford OHS. However, her true passion lies in interdisciplinary research and women's issues. At 16, she worked with professors and graduate students at the University of California, Santa Barbara, and was first author to a research paper titled, "Law and Order: The Weaponisation of Rape and Post-Conflict Disenfranchisement of Bosnian Women." She has also contributed research to developers of a Sexual Assault Forensics Bill, that is to be presented at the Prime Minister's Office in Delhi. In line with this research, Vedika has been invited as a Keynote Speaker for the Lion's District Conference and 100-year commemoration. She has also spoken at the Indo- American Society and received honors from both institutions.

Outside of academics, Vedika is especially passionate about art. In 2016, two of her artworks were selected to centre the Stanford OHS Magazine and in 2018 she was selected for a solo art exhibition at the National Centre of Performing Arts in Mumbai. In wake of research and travel experiences, she focused pieces from this exhibition on the individual voice: each painting is inspired by someone else's story. All proceeds went towards mental health counselling and art therapy programs at local hospitals.